The Tattoo Collector

The Tattoo Collector

Tim Tim Cheng

Nine
Arches
Press

The Tattoo Collector
Tim Tim Cheng

ISBN: 978-1-916760-04-2
eISBN: 978-1-916760-05-9

First published October 2024 by:

Nine Arches Press
Unit 14, Sir Frank Whittle Business Centre,
Great Central Way, Rugby.
CV21 3XH
United Kingdom

www.ninearchespress.com

Printed on recycled paper in the United Kingdom by Imprint Digital.

Nine Arches Press is supported using public funding
by Arts Council England.

Supported using public funding by
ARTS COUNCIL ENGLAND

Contents

III.

Questions for the Police at Royal Infirmary

Am I making too much eye contact

Do you always work nights

What will I have for breakfast

Did you know the coffee machine does not work

Should I look at those old ladies' bruised faces

Are you sick of your job

Why am I looking at you without disgust

Is it because this country is so new to me

Do you think soap operas use the right props for your badges

Did you call the police as a kid

Was it a prank or a threat

What makes you talk: the lack of windows or the colour grey

If you were in the interrogation room, could you tell my great granny lied

Are you kind when no one watches

I.

"A sense of being responsible for a crisis may also give a feeling of control."

– *Empathy*, Mei-mei Berssenbrugge (1989)

The Tattoo Collector

Incisions, incisions, incisions –
Gloved fingers stretch my skin for the ink to set.
I'm convinced if I turn my blank slate
into a puzzle, an exhibit, you'll be looking
and not looking into me, a site for stencilling
future's blueprints. I've practised letting strangers
apply pressure on me. Elbow my shoulders
as they resist the coming of black outlines,
which safeguard every lost charm –
a swallow faces a mountain it can never reach.
Needs to needles. Blessed are the pains
that numb other pains: I kneel on a butterfly
with time's spiral as wings. Close by, a naked night-
rider gallops the pitch dark. Her eyes glow, hair flies.

Surgeons' Hall Museum

You are an animal seeking structures
    A structure seeking animals
        Animals your shattered facts
            Shattered facts your animals

Death allows a love too violent for the living
    The living, a violent love of death
        Violence lets live in the afterlife
            The afterlife lets in

Your feet are weak from the silence of saws
    The silence of what you saw
        A foot snapped, bound heel-shaped
            Fissured into rot

You desire some biography
    Some reads *bandaged, aged six*
        You are like those who desired her jiggly gait
            Named that lotus feet

You name a woman by her suffering
    A woman names you her suffering
        Which you inherit without knowing
            Without her knowing

Skin. Me.

Here a black star that stops smudging
was someone's shoulder, now a waxy
bookmark. Here a snake that hisses at
its eternal reflection was someone's
chest. Laurel leaves anchor a boat
between faded nipples. Hair floats
around them in formalin. Here you
fantasise about being skinned, hung
whole in a glass box. Your thigh, a
pantry of food tattoos, cracking with
lines of a leather couch: ramen spilling
from tumultuous soup, a muscular,
blue mushroom, a pomegranate
halved next to a grumpy, clothed
avocado drinking from a nonic pint.
Here you are, of clothes, of skin, of
sinews, of bones, of nothing away
from other visitors, flipping the big
book. Gratitude, in many hands, is
incomplete. If you count people in jars
too, the hall gets crowded. Here, the
more marked you are the easier it is to
identify

                              you.

Sometimes, you are at the wrong party

A note in Cantopop can't be found in other music.
It's a girl convincing herself *it is what it is*.
Friends may forgive you by saying
drinking and travelling are ways
to self-medicate, while you want to punch
and get a refund from everyone
who encourages you to dream bigger.

> A classmate says *if I were from your background,*
> *I would not make it here.* Another says
> *everyone should have a three-year plan.*
> So every three years, you quit your job,
> rack up student loans, delete your Instagram.

It's not too late. Let quiet fill your room
with the mothers you were afraid of becoming –
Yours used to visit a pawnshop monthly,
thumbing cash from a raised counter.
When she redeemed her jewellery, she smiled
as if you would never return again.

Master Narratives

In the graveyard, we know not to pick bluebells
but I step on a snail. The sun hushes.
Behind Burton's sandstone tent of a tomb
is a stair to look in. Glare on scratched glass.
Bones invisibly bedded on two ends.
Isabel burned her husband's last books,
hoping they would taste good. In their image,
I translate my flesh into empires, possessed
by *the thing* that also reads as 東西 *eastwest.*
Why do I still believe – like a stranger –
that being understood could save us?
As moss eats into benches, statues,
nameless headstones, we watch our steps,
watch for that faint crushing of shells.

The Tattooist

The Dutch soldiers came with tobacco,
            the Japanese with brothels.
Long before their arrivals
                        we had always sharpened our teeth,
      lining, webbing our limbs
            with sugarcane juice and soot.

                        Mallets broke bits of our bodies
            to prepare us for a husband, prevent us
                  from being abducted
                        as comfort women.

      To bear fate on our skins, our skins,
   our bearing, housing our souls –
a graphite starburst on my shoulder
            sheltered me from evils
      lurking in the jungle, the way
                  raindrops bounce from petals.

                  In assigned villages far from our forest,
                        I dreamt. My grandmother
                  smoked a big, fat cigar. Her hands
            dotted like the prickly fronds
                  she lived among. She told me

            for every drop of blood
                  spilled onto the ground
            an earthquake will ensue.

They better do.

My Bloody Galentines

i.

Everytime I hold a balloon I shake it like my own head
or pretend it is my pregnant belly.
Not that I have plans. It is just a thing I was brought up
to imagine: my body could house another body.
When time is ripe, it will push itself through me
like I am a river that parts to make way.

ii.

My girl friends give everyone a balloon.
Praises and our names stretch across their milky skin
holding gold flakes and air. Our balloons stutter
around the room for which I have no name,
shocked by the size of this house. Every cupboard
feels like a door to a room I should not enter.

iii.

Plates and flutes on the carpet are listening to us:
for every new bone we find in a creek,
we'll find more from forgotten times –
Landscapes framed on the wall are too pale –
I could almost taste the ghosts of those girls.
I could almost taste the ghosts of those girls.

Girl Ghosts

say Surabaya. Sound like eight again. Girl ghosts pick and choose their countries. Yes to father's nose, mother's eyes. No to her wiggling pair of lí zi, her widowed, high-pitched *lǎo lǐ, lǎo lǐ.* Girl ghosts beat each other into meat floss. Shout *luun daak,* the only Hokkien girl ghosts pass on. Be it Surabaya or Putien, girl ghosts are rich, beautiful, in denial. Love being loved by landlord fathers. Steam thin rice cakes when the rice runs out. Charge neighbours for watching their TV. Girl ghosts are crying. Girl ghosts are not crying. Girl ghosts are learning èrhú in Fuzhou. Hands, frost-bitten, out of tune. The èrhú cries out for girl ghosts with long faces, low registers. Girl ghosts don't think xìqǔ schools like them. Girl ghosts drop singing. Raise girl ghosts in Hong Kong. Girl ghosts meet in a tea restaurant with a beauty pageant play set. Porcelain clatters among girl ghost chatters. Girl ghosts want to be the champion. An uncle tells girl ghosts *Champion? More like pork chops!* Girl ghosts tell girl ghosts *Study hard. Compensate for having your father's small eyes!* Girl ghosts take group photos. Swipe other girl ghosts out of the screen. Girl ghosts enlarge themselves in part: Face. Hair. Belly. Girl ghosts suck the eyes out of fish heads with fermented soy beans. The heads of girl ghosts fly out of stuffed winter melons.

Jades / 国

Today we can't say the word *jade*.   翠
A leader thinks its radicals read like

his name dying twice,
as if speech act was dark magic:

do not practise flying.   羽
Choose between being pawns   卒

or an abrupt end. Some news ago,
a man almost killed himself,

shoving a raw jade melon up his arse.
When I learned about homophobia,

I started to enjoy
jade melon dishes again,

especially the seeds
that soak up all the good sauce.

A true visionary, the man
who keeps living the jade suicide

every time someone thinks of him.

Blue Fires

Have you forgotten the fires

Have you forgotten the fires
The fires remember

Have you forgotten the fires
The fires remember
I sit next to an elder whose hand is scorched into a clenched claw

Have you forgotten the fires
The fires remember
I sit next to an elder whose hand is scorched into a clenched claw
She says flames do not cast shadows

Have you forgotten the fires
The fires remember
I sit next to an elder whose hand is scorched into a clenched claw
She says flames do not cast shadows

She never says so but I need somewhere
To place the memory my body rejects

It is hotter than what is visible. Therefore, blue

Derek Jarman says before you turn blind, the world turns blue

Blue is drumming in my arms
Blue is drumming in my arms
Blue is drumming in my arms
Blue is drumming in my arms

Molotovs manifest what is bottled up

I prefer confrontation to catharsis
What could be to what is
Experience to nostalgia

I am about to touch the fire inside me
And find the fire you touched

Emergency Regulations Ordinance (1922-)

Mr. CHURCHILL A further telegram was received from the Governor of Hong Kong yesterday afternoon. [*she was next to me*] He reports that as the strike has spread to butchers, bakers, domestic servants. [*i ran away*] [H]e issued Proclamations on the 25th February prohibiting persons from leaving the Colony without passes (with the object of retaining necessary labour in the Colony). [*when the baton hit her head*] [...] Domestic servants and also the staff of many firms and some Government servants, such as office messengers, have come out. [*i can't sleep*] The engineers guild, including practically all mechanics, are to come out to-day. [*don't say you're sorry for us*] The printers struck on Saturday. The Governor reports with regret that a large body of strikers came into collision with Indian troops [there's *no time to cry*] who fired four shots and killed three men, wounding several others. [...] [*when you're on the frontline*] I have not sufficient information about what is going on in Hong Kong to be able to give a definite answer at the present time. [*you can't wake*] I should have thought that, judging from the hon. and gallant Member's views in other directions, the policy of conscription of labour would have excited his enthusiasm in Hong Kong as much as it does in Russia. [*those who feign sleep*] Mr. STEWART In view of the very peaceable nature of the people, [*i'm not going home*] so far as I know them, would the right hon. Gentleman say that these intimidations are the result of Bolshevik propaganda? [*i can't*]

What do you do with a stone?

Lick it? Crack walnuts? Find more and pile them up?

A monkey broke a glass enclosure with a stone at a zoo.

After the act, the monkey stepped back and ran away.

Perhaps it looked surprised. Perhaps it was more curious than rebellious.

Perhaps it was more intelligent than other monkeys in the same captivity.

Did others follow suit (before all stones were removed)?

How do we tell intent and instincts apart?

I do not want to conflate or understate the bonds between living things.

After protesters fell to their death, glass shards sparkled along road cracks.

Streets were unpaved to build brick-henges, an architecture of deferral.

Blunt tools ticked, ticked, ticking to reveal the sand beneath.

(So this is how the city is built –

On *the determination to own destruction!*)

When general strikes paralysed the traffic – by means of walking in and
out of train doors incessantly together, or moving furniture onto highways,
bridges – spectacles were translated back into streets.

A sofa at a crossroad looked inwards at thick crowds:

A lady cried on her way to work: *what don't you understand?*

A seething black creature pointed its many scraped fingers at her:

what don't you understand?

A protester came forward to lead the lady away.

Faces and Masks

after Eduardo Galeano (1984)

1834: Mexico City

A calabash
filled with vinegar mounts
guard behind each door.
On every altar a thousand candles
pray.
Doctors prescribe bloodlettings and
chloride fumigations.
Coloured flags
mark houses invaded by the plague.
Lugubrious streets
with nobody on them.
The governor issues
a proclamation banning
certain foods.
According to him,
stuffed chilis and fruits
have brought cholera
to Mexico.
On Holy Ghost Street,
a coachman is cutting an enormous
chirimoya. He stretches out
from his perch to enjoy
eating it bit by bit.
Someone passing by
leaves him with his mouth open.
"Barbarian! Don't you see
you're committing suicide?
Don't you know that
that fruit takes you to the grave?

2019: HKSAR

No lessons. We gathered
at the library. Officials
showed up late on screens,
sipping water before the press
conference on the mask ban.
You clenched your teeth, swore,
talked back. Dumbstruck
on friends' shoulders.
National birthday still itched
in my throat –
ashened roadblocks, exhaust,
leers from passersby who could
only breathe through hands –
Being young wasn't a crime.
Knowing and showing was.
I stayed at the library
to read with you.
You, born in the year of SARS,
as old as the face masks
in my drawers. You, said
to make up a student body
too small for job markets.
You, who marched drumming
with earphones attached
to Taiyo fish sausage.
There you were, saving me
from this world's unmasking,
with a patience so wild
it bit half-dried cement.

The Birth of a New Hero

after Tung Ming-Chin (2008)

When they cut you down,
I bend my knees,
curl up into a camphor tree stump.
A second skin envelops me,
softening edges.
I cover my face with both hands.
Their honesty breathes.
I crack, ripple where my joints jut.
Forget costless nicety.
Forget proud annihilation.
Forget how life goes on.
Here's to searchlights
storming through households,
replacing dawns.
Here's to shadows now statues.
To unblinking mornings.
That acute quiet in our bread,
our bite-sized offering.

How Memory Works

on the sudden closure of Apple Daily, the biggest pro-democracy press in Hong Kong

i.

We see the newspaper for tomorrow, not tomorrow,
it's already midnight. Today that is. News that stays
warm and inky on our fingertips at 2:30 a.m.

ii.

I keep thinking of a kong girl last year this time,
one among the thousands staying up to queue,
to stream: her black T-shirt, hot pants, flip flops.

iii.

Printers rumble and spit beyond the usual volume.
Papers snake along conveyor belts, up and down,
all over the factory. The ASMR of holding fast.

iv.

Sure they won't catch us for buying the paper?
Mother went with me, still. *Ghosts police too.*
She prayed only for me to hear.

v.

I would love to believe the sky
is apologising but it never does.
We rain on its behalf.

vi.

In convenience stores:
Cashier A: "It's not here yet" without looking.
Cashier B: "How many copies?" without counting.

vii.

Newspapers are a genre for fathers.
They die again with the newspaper.
Their absence, the absence of words.

viii.

Tat Ming Pair: *why is this person making me*
ask for the only choice in this garden?
I picked a formless fruit, already forbidden.

ix.

Windowless: news about news. Bars behind bars.
Forms of Farewell: stare straight. Hit and miss.
Sounds and fury. Refresh – 404 not found.

x.

We saved interviews and unphotogenic snaps,
the mean, low-cost animations too.
We mourn every day. We are good at it now.

Reiki

I sat next to Pamela, waiting
for our friends to call it a day,

for the Mihn club to open.
She put her palms together,

barely blinked, focused
on somewhere beyond

the shop window. Outside,
the dark alley a mirror:

I asked if she was meditating.
She said no, lifting one hand –

a card, written with names: the couple's,
(their cat's too) and the hospital's.

She invited me to place my palm
in the space between hers.

"I'm sending energy to the wife.
She's due tomorrow… she's so

tiny… you know." "I know…
been following the husband's

letters from the prison."
My shoulders loosened in the warmth.

I stopped talking to make room,
thinking of an infant's playdough fist

tight around a mother's finger,
insulated by a big wish.

Rudimentary Cantonese

for Shawn Shawn

Your toddler's accent renews tong^4 si^1,
poems from the Tang Dynasty,
gracing anxious aunties before sleep
who play your videos on repeat.

Lines	*now live*	*beyond the poet's intention.*
花落 faa^1 lok^6	final	最終 / flowers fall
知 zi^1	擳	tickle / who knows
多少 do^1 siu^2	到笑	smile / how many?

Your mother goes by the name Zi,
knowing *he'll be as stubborn as me.*
"H" stands for home, Hong Kong
but more importantly, honesty.

You will soon gain a new tongue.
Cantonese may just live among
your household, in the tilted rhymes
of springs sleeping in mind's soil.

MAJESTY

WWT London Wetland Centre, June 2022

I keep saying Jubilee as Jollibee,
meal deals preferred to monarchy.

The sky has never been this messy:
Scared by air parades, birds flee.

Death Accents

You are wanted, the moon elder and government announced, *drawing red threads*.

The night the Pillar of Shame was dismembered, I scrolled my way home and texted you. *In the thumbnail, the pillar looked like a slice of pizza.* I never liked those shades of rust and burn, struggling torsos with hollows, molten, torn skyward.

I preferred the pillar's absence. The outline of its base, a square lighter than its surrounding, spoke louder. Homemade palm-sized pillars spoke louder, too. Another way to spell *ideas* was *die as*.

When I met the artist of the Pillar of Shame, we did not talk. When an audience member asked, he said *the government's reaction was part of his performance.*

Anne Carson wrote: *Shame requires the eyes of others unlike guilt.*

On the same panel, Cantonese, Burmese, Thai accents beamed with confidence, in confidence. *Make your own loyalty cards. Redeem something on your tenth arrest.* I wanted to flirt with fear, too.

Mother decided for me that a BN(O) passport was too pricey. Its forms, too long. Still, I moved to a country called writing. My Hong Kong numbers became passwords. Security, an echo.

The diaspora split into the witness and witnessed. Homesick. Sick of home. People back home did not need the diaspora.

The night you came to visit, you spoke of actions unreported, uncharged. Repercussions were concentric. The inner rings, quiet triumphs. The outer rings, noisy defeats. Did our feet touch under the table?

Longing was my first way to love. Shame made me think it was the only way.

A red dot crawled across the book in my hands. I turned the page – a red trail where words were not.

II.

"They, lands of the accumulated ferocious secretions that we name history, for lack of a better word."

– *Sea and Fog*, Etel Adnan (2012)

After *Isla*

The sea hisses *elsewhere, elsewhere,* as I let go
of the illusion of safety, where
land is land.

      My body pierces the low sky.
Its creased syllables

           become hooks
coated in rust,

        in angry sugar and blood.

        The sea speaks all and nothing.
      The sea speaks all and nothing. I,

a territory of wants,

           riddled into fish.

Lantau (Rotten Head)

i.

"The day a calf was halved by a propeller,
white dolphins poked at its remains
as if it was still swimming,
the sea, its CPR, its heartbeat."

Where did I read that –
most mammals can't fully process death:
some mothers carry the child's body
until they learn grief is lighter to keep.

ii.

How much would you pay
for catches, daughters and songs,
their makings defined
by their distance from the shore.

iii.

"A fisherwoman who hated seafood
knew her catch by heart,
by the strength and angle it bit
into her hooks. By the same logic,

she tied her children to a pole
when the sea was hungry – her husband
too dead to do so, limbs tangled
with mooring lines, drawn in, unawares."

iv.

There's a reason why, in Cantonese,
soeng[5] ngon[6], *getting to the shore*
could mean getting an apartment,
which is to say, you were settled.

v.

Songs couldn't send us back
to sailing routes. Still we sang
to reach you in pieces.
When land once water and islets

recalled our unmapped names,
would you rise,
would you find yourself
in lineages of endurance –

vi.

Falcons circled overhead, a buzzing
drone among them. Here, on these islands,
butchers processed no livestock
but histories. Vacation houses stood

hollower than prisons and asylums.
This water kept changing hands. It began
where our cities inched into sand.
Between the words *sink* and *sunk*,

there's a vision without us.

The Sand I Stand On Is Not My Own

Measure the ways continents reshape:
by tonnes, by months, by artificial islands.
Colossal metal serpents dredge and suck
seafloors in a bubbly slurry.
Rivers blazed into mud puddles.
Coasts recede. Graveyards regurgitate bones
by the shore as vessels bob, spitting curves
of dirt stolen, smuggled, sold from nations
to nations for a nation of promises
that break the ones in existence. The sand
I stand on is not my own but a congregation
of distances. Where my room now is, there
was none. I still take it, nothing strategic,
the way dead things settle in sediments.

The Tattoo Collector

He wasn't the first to say *I really like your*
jellyfish. I didn't know it reached
from your spine all the way down your thighs.

Thanks, I said, *It's not the most obvious thing*
when you first meet a person.

From bed to café, our faces looked different.
I thought of facing a fallen tree:
its robust aerial roots, my hair loosening

from a bun, the jellyfish on my back
formed an orgy of symmetries.

He liked it when I told him
I was grading papers with a red pen
as my blood seeped through tattoo needles

– a marble marriage
with swirling tentacles.

Deluge

All this rain, as if the sky is falling
into our arms.

In a myth, we are children of Lo Ting,
a half-human, half-fish.

In another, salt revolts in our blood.
It cannot be taxed.

Our mountain's name is the proof:
dai⁶ yu⁴, *big fish, big rain* at a slant.

We move from what gives life.
It calls for our return in structures

small, sudden, this-that soundproof:
doors can't keep the water out.

Trains, an aquarium of strange fish –
news from the Mainland leaks.

I could've been one of the casualties
had mother not moved to Hong Kong,

where ridicules on anything Chinese,
deaths included, are the few things

we could claim control.
About Zhengzhou, a place that shares

my absent father's surname,
all I know is a singer's raspy voice,

censored, mulling over the loss
of someone, somewhere, something

that dissipates in direct gaze.
Where is the singer now?

How many drowned?
I need to write about something else

like mist after rain.

Field Notes

North East New Territories, Hong Kong

FROM THE SOIL

We make our son. From the soil we make our son biscuits. From the soil we make our son biscuits stored in ceramic bowls. From the soil we make our son biscuits stored in ceramic bowls made with the same soil. From the soil we make our son biscuits stored in ceramic bowls made with the same soil we dig, burn, grind into red dusts. From the soil we make our son biscuits stored in ceramic bowls made with the same soil we dig, burn, grind into *red dusts*, which means *earthly affairs*, a dream in an utterance that presupposes us.

DAY TRIPS

Your son tugs at my sleeve, making me get him the red sugar cubes you prepared for our tea. Zest and mint. He knows I'm eager to please but you notice. So you push away the red sugar cubes and give him biscuits instead. The biscuits look like tiny pebbles. "These are sweet too." Tiny fingers. Tiny bites. He is always eating. The way he abandoned his bread in the bookshelf for play last time we visited. This farm, this house, his birthplace: layered red soil, ghosts, and labour in the bathtub. Sweet when taken in small doses.

GIVE AND TAKE

Take the mugwort and rub it on your skin. Take the lemongrass spray. The bugs are used to us. We are used to the bugs. They could tell you are new here so they go at you. Take the tomatoes. It's not a harvest, it's an explosion from the unbroken rain. I have been eating them, *only* eating them for a week. Take the white corn. Eat them raw. A burst of sunshine. Take Luk Sum. Take Man Gor. Take Ling Tai. Take Fai Gei. Take Tong San. Take Ling Jie. Take other farmers in mind, too. Oh, don't forget the last batch of tofu from a friend's closing factory.

STRANGENESS

Mud potatoes. Hermit potatoes. Gone potatoes. Fingered potatoes. Starch-maze potatoes. Potatoes turned metal turned potatoes. Care potatoes. Performance potatoes. Pepper-sprayed potatoes. Postscript potatoes. Guilt potatoes. Distraction potatoes. Designedly powerless potatoes. Cottage-core potatoes. Plough-before-noon potatoes. Couch potatoes. Out-of-sync potatoes. Navel-gazing potatoes. Quote unquote potatoes. Fictionally non-fictional fiction potatoes. First-person past potatoes. Trust-worthy potatoes.

TRUST

"Our son was born before dawn. We named him Hei Yeung, *hope for the sun*. I never quite trusted the hospital. We read and discussed with each other to decide on the bathtub. The what-ifs became shared. Not all of us agreed. The ones who stayed in the farmhouse helped my home birth." "We do talk about everything, like the way we share our income: wage or taking from the communal safe when needed?" "Sometimes we lose friends with the same belief, who want it differently." "But I know they're out there, working."

TO YIELD

Serve – sever; our – out: gunshots from unseen barracks puncture the air. Some doors do not open in the village, not just these vintage cars before us but always the fire, always the bulldozer razing the soil before it is taken from your hands. Farmers without farms. The city that no longer feeds itself collapses into your throat. "My tears sell better than my crops, eh?" Your mind, your body yields to the soil, despite – the day a friend's farm shuts down, another celebrates a tiny harvest. Rice stalks bend slightly, giving.

Salt and Rice

between a Cantonese father and daughter

How much salt have you eaten over the years
to make you always state the opposite
with a grain of salt? How many grains of salt
do you need to fill up your *salt shakers*,
your *dignity*? Does your daily dignity lie
in how *you have had more salt than my having rice*?
You can't eat democracy like rice, you say,
hands stop, mouth stops, a job is a job.
Can you still translate a day job as *find eat*
if you are skipping lunch for work? If work
can't guarantee *safety, joy, tea and rice*,
why shouldn't we rise? *We? rise?* Do *we* really
read as *everyone*? Some do prefer rolling
as salt in waves to being crystallised.

Future Perfect

I used to steal pens from my mother's **place** · smell their silicone
grips · like I was at hers again · I created little time loops · counting
down · *in a few days · I will have returned to my grandmother's · thinking
of the moment I* **thought** *of this* · as I turned the pen **below my nose**
· snorting · sorting needs I could not name · the future patted me
on the shoulder · humming *you are you are prepared for grief* · I used
to steal pens from my mother's place · **smell their silicone** grips ·
like I was at hers again · I created little time loops · counting down
· *in a few days · I will have returned to* **my** *grandmother's · thinking of
the moment I thought of this* · as I turned the pen below my nose ·
snorting · sorting needs I could not name · the future patted me
on the shoulder · humming *you are you are prepared for grief* · I used
to steal pens from **my** mother's place · smell their silicone grips ·
like I was at hers again · I created little time loops · counting down
· *in a few days · I will have returned to my grandmother's · thinking of
the moment I thought of this* · as I turned the pen below my nose ·
snorting · sorting needs I could not name · the future patted me
on the shoulder · humming *you are you are prepared for grief* · I used
to steal pens from my mother's place · smell their silicone **grips** ·
like I was at hers again · I created little time loops · counting down
· *in a few days · I will have returned to my grandmother's · thinking of
the moment I thought of this* · as I turned the pen below my nose ·
snorting · sorting needs I could not name · the future patted me
on the shoulder · humming *you are you are prepared for grief* · I used
to steal pens from my mother's place · smell their silicone grips ·
like I was at hers again · I created little **time** loops · counting down
· *in a few days · I will have returned to my grandmother's · thinking of
the moment I thought of this* · as I turned the pen below my nose ·
snorting · sorting needs I could not name · the future patted me
on the shoulder · humming *you are you are prepared for grief* · I used
to steal pens from my mother's place · smell their silicone grips ·
like I was at hers again · I created little time loops · counting down

· in a few days · I will have returned to my grandmother's · thinking of the moment I thought of this · as I turned the pen below my nose · snorting · sorting need**s** I could not name · the future patted me on the shoulder · humming *you are you are pre**pare**d for grief·* I used to steal pens from my mother's place · smell their silicone grips · like I was at hers again · I created little ti**me** loops · counting down *· in a few days · I will have returned to my grandmother's · thinking of the moment I thought of this ·* as I turned the pen below my nose · snorting · sorting need**s** I could not name · the future patted me on the shoulder · humming *you are you are pre**pare**d for grief·* I used to steal pens from my mother's place · smell their silicone grips · like I was at hers again · I created little time loops · counting down *· in a few days · I will have returned to **my** grandmother's · thinking of the moment I thought of this ·* as I turned the pen below my nose · snorting · sorting **needs** I could not name · the future patted me on the shoulder · humming *you are you are prepared for grief·* I used to steal pens from my mother's place · smell their silicone grips · like I was at hers again · I created little time loops · counting down *· in a few days · I will have returned to my grandmother's · thinking of the moment I thought of this ·* as I turned the pen below my nose ·

Entrails

Granny gave each of us a yellow rubber duck,
the kind you imagine yourself squeezing in the bathtub.
Mine settled on her chest, on the shoreline between
a blue blanket and chequered pyjamas.
They must have been worn and taken off
from patients of her deflating size.

*

Sometimes, there was more than one slimy pool
on the dining room's floor.
Granny would beat and pull the pale
pig intestines coiled in plastic basins,
sitting on a stool too small for her hips.

The mustiness would waft
as she stuffed fistfuls of dried oysters,
seaweed, aniseed-spiced sticky rice
into carefully cleaned casings.

*

Your mother screams a lot at night,
Granny told the next-bed family, *me too.*

I went downstairs to buy her a tabloid.
It was too wordy a distraction
from the orchestral practices of pain.

*

Granny would sew those 'duor leng mui' –
my ears can't catch their Hokkien twang –
and fry them in peanut oil's gossip.
They were tasty despite being
chewy, soapy.

*

She doesn't make this dish now, not because
her sons-in-law were appalled
by the dozen boiled pig stomachs,
boxes of mandarins, bags and bags
under the table that took hours to clear.

It has more to do with what she calls –
a joke with her nurse – xiǎo dìdi (her weenie
or her colon), all its raw movements
bulging next to her belly button.

瑞龍樓 Shui Lung House

Granny jogs and jogs down the corridor,
stomping, panting past neighbours' doors.
Her song thunders far to near,
near to far.

小羊乖乖

Granny, granny, please, come home.
Great granny is asking why
the kids outside are now under our table.
Her muddy eyes are bulging like a pug's.

把門開開

A batik dress, hung from the ceiling fan,
turns and turns in the dining room.
Behind the always shut green curtain:
mothballs, steamed vinegar, faeces.

快點開開

Granny, granny, please, come home.
Edges are knifelike in street lights.
Something slithers by my wrist,
strangles great granny as she sleeps.

媽媽回來了

The Tattoo Collector

A nurse gave me candy for not crying at the jab –
I take the same pride holding my breath

as I lie naked before my tattooists.
Ceaseless, mechanical buzzes fill the room.

One of their needles goes deeper
than the other into the skin of my belly,

the different strengths between
bold clouds searing across my ribs,

eagles' feathers dotted
by the metallic fang near my navel –

some say the clouds and eagles hurt the same
but this skin hears one at a time.

Florence and the Machine

I   too   want to be a mermaid   hold my breath
in ocean   as long as the notes you sustain
stained glass breaks   into a choir   of you
looking up   beyond spotlights

The best I could do is   dye my hair red
and sing in the shower   longing is guttural
instants scramble   out of my throat
werewolves dash across tundras   to shudder

in the bathwater   the best chorus is
just a cry   before that   ghosts must whistle
like boiling kettles   how much wonder is
in a gasp   elation is neck-snapping

You jump and jump still   a bright splash of bird
shit on your foot   your panting
raw rhythms   wrists   stirring the air
beat tides in my blood

What if the hardest thing   is to whisper
rest assured   you're heard
to learn not to be afraid of sighing   sighs
that breathe   into all that is hurt

Yau Teng Daughters

A yau teng daughter is an open secret. They lower their voices to call her
a *sick* daughter, an *oil lamp* daughter, a *boat* daughter.

> *Already sick* – her new family is not responsible.

> *An oil lamp* – she reads shadows in the room until she can't say *daddy*.

> *A boat* – half of family reunions steer away from her.

They'll meet at daddy's funeral for the first and only time. It won't be the first
time daddy dies: in a blurry photo, she sees a man who shares her moon face.

Her granny tells her to *keep this from your mum*. Her mum tells her to *keep this
from your granny*. They both say men aren't trustworthy.

This isn't why she can't call her mum's husband *daddy*. She sees through it
when her mum says *his surname is different from yours because… he changed it.*

Surnames are elegies. She never took his. She didn't like the idea of sounding
like a *desk* daughter although she was as good as a *desk* –

> *A desk* so huge it'd be strange to sit right next to or across from each other.

Sometimes, she looks at the mirror to tie what she feels to her face. To touch
is to close the distance. Sex seems more natural than a hug.

> *Listen again*: the secrets open like legs.

Waterlogged

from Hong Kong to Edinburgh

Cloud puffs hovered below,
their shadows above red tile roofs.

      Vapour condensed on windows,
      straining to contain

the bird's eye view of everything,
faintly outlined in English books.

      How much rain must I hold
      if I were to make this language

I've lived outside, scratched at,
mine? The day I landed,

      the city greeted me:
      raindrops in a stranger's copper hair.

A Small Book of Distance

Mother asked for some light reading
in Chinese. I lent her books I liked at thirteen,
surprised by the intimacy of knowing each other
halfway on the page. How did she
go from peeking at my diary, alarmed
by the emo lyrics I copied
to this? I had been hiding behind English,
something she picked up selling tourists clothes,
never fluent enough to read me.
I seemed to have sneaked out
to find her whole with yearnings.

To find her,
I sneaked out of schools
fluent enough
to sell bread
in English.
I copied *I'm good, have a good one*
from colleagues, alarmed
as I met my mother halfway
as immigrants.
最近好忙, I replied sometimes
when she asked if I was okay.

III.

……那永久 飄零的
卵子的天性
是叛亂

—曹疏影《她的小舌尖時時救我》(2021)

Re: *Do you feel guilty for not writing in your mother tongue?*

We are in a field. The grass is unruly.

I stand holding a mirror. My torso is out of view.

To you, the field is tunnelling through me.

The views behind and before me merge.

I serve the mirror that frames the field that frames the mirror.

Between the field and the mirror, the grass is already something else.

All that grammar and glimmer.

For the grass to reach the mirror, you cannot be proximate.

It is generous. Both of us, almost missing.

We seem not to go or stay.

The Tattoo Collector

Strange how tattoos stay on mummies.
The flesh beneath dissolves
but the skin remains embalmed,
markings intact:

those brief, horizontal lines
charcoal-inked on Ötzi's body,
unearthed from a glacier
five-thousand years since death

by an arrow wound in his shoulder.
No one knows for sure
if the lines are medical or not
but today, slightly after Ötzi's recovery,

you say you've decided
on plum blossoms and branches
along your legs, where rashes
sometimes bloom:

the tattooist must observe
your erratic dapples for hours
to design something lasting,
to capture your skin's weather.

Eczema

i.

Blossoms terrify me.
Gaping, they let out their interior
without shame, as if asking
why can't you be as open?

Now my skin is ripening with them.
This thin colony itches, peeling.
Sloughed scales cover my couch,
floating by bright windows.

I can smell my immunity,
sweet as a stranger. To scratch
is to turn myself inside out,
defying borders.

ii.

Inside ziplock bags, dry gardens crunch:
snake chunks, citrus peels,
cicada molts, shrubs, bark slices
sealed by the clinic's cross,
my patient's barcode.

With three bowls of tap water,
I stew such ancient contents
into a swamp best served warm.
As I down the throat-drying bitterness,
its yellow-rimmed crescent stagnates,

thick with dregs at the bottom of my bowl.
To heal is trial and error –
no cream, no pills this time,
just some prunes in crumpled wrappers,
their sticky tang to get me through.

Skye-ward

i.

Your train passes a valley –

Mountains around you
are unnamable muscles.

Your insides
shift like sand
as animals go ashore.

Their scars, blinding
as snow
tearing through spring.

ii.

What if crags and calm
are synonyms:

shaved tops chitter
to bitten stacks.

Fat folds climax
into spired charm.

iii.

The rapture of moss:

seeing its curbside self
magnify
over mountain belts,

as if every plant
is a borrowed thought.

The colour
between black, brown, yellow, green
is called clarity.

What Have You Thrown Away

Edinburgh, 2022

The city has answered my prayer – half a tangerine jabbed on a spear-top railing
    – I wanted free fruits peeled, bite-sized, package-less.

Miscellaneous cores, rinds loll between ventilation grilles to the side of an alley.
    Did someone put them there? Did the building throw up?

Like a lean rat the street split and skinned, a pomegranate dangles
    between a rugged wall and oxidised pipe, where one seed sticks.

Seagulls, stronger and louder during bin strikes, arise immaculately
    from busted melons, a sweet mulch by the roadside.

Sometimes, I think, my love for displaced things is just another form
    of self-talk: *there's no such thing as nowhere. I see you.*

Salvaging

In sunshowered Orkney, rainbows sprouted after I failed to withdraw cash. What a thing. To spend all my money to be in nature. To be in nature when I could not drive. According to the tour guide, *a boy once saw a soldier jump from a ship. From afar, the boy thought: that seems fun. I wanna join him.* Oil spilt along ice shards. Frozen water burned. Causes of death did not offset each other – as such, I replied to emails after encircling the Ring of Brodgar, wind-chewed moss sandwiches. The circles were complete. Back on the tour bus, an upturned ladybug struggled. *One had to turn shipwrecks upside down to dispatch them from town to town. Rumoured, too, to have been reused for satellites.* From sea to space, their ageless steel orbited our moonlit purposes. I sat with opposites, an empty seat, and looked out.

The Fo(u)rth Bridge

I came across the bridge you photographed and sent me,
(which you thought looked like the one back home,
five-thousand nine-hundred and eleven miles away).
I almost missed it, dozing off on the bus – but the bridge
to my right was a harp burning bright.
Three bridges stand parallel, immense at sea,
each built a century apart: the one to my left
was half-engulfed in the dark, its red oxide tentacles
knotting into fans of steel.
                            The night you asked me
to *look at the sparks firing off that bridge*
under construction! It was one a.m., the police ignored us
(two adults, not street kids, sharing sushi bentos,
a convenience store luxury) by the reclaimed harbour.
I was all eyes on everything, except your face, except
those few seconds at your loose brows, highball-blush.
Of all the straight things straight people juggled,
straight talk eluded me: it's easier to say
we can use my face to sell the underwear you wear
than to say *I want to build something with you.*

Hiking, we

turned to see they are far behind.
We didn't go too fast, the first thing
you said to me, always a few steps ahead.
You warned of tippy planks on muddy stairs
as I plodded sandy incline with toes too tense,
not wanting to, but what if you could hear me
pant, squeal at tricky spots.

We crawled through a fallen tree's tunnel
to Lai Chi Wo Village, the irony
of blessings on frayed spring couplets.
There were no ghosts but collapsed rooftops,
our sweat-soaked hair. *Someone's trapped
in the narrow alley between brick houses.*
I almost believed, the way

a typhoon pounded persistently
as I waited alone in his tent.
My spine singed
with the tent's swishing fabric
as pines thrashed on Mount Naeba.
I was waiting for him to be back, to unzip
the mosquito net first, tooth by tooth.

Boyfriend for Scale

after Maggie Smith's Wife for Scale

History is wild grass peeking out
through earth-coloured ruins –

tourists gather like toothache
at the mouth of old traps,

the spikes of which are rusty
from search dogs and enemies.

The always-retiring tour guide asks us
to pose next to a phallic statue.

He looks at me, smirking.
What does this stone look like?

We're the last interracial couple he asks,
as if he wants to be entertained too.

It is and is not a lie when I say
a thumbs-up magnified. A photo I take

does show you raising your thumb
by the rock, which is your size.

Tell me: if I said *it's a human-sized dick,
just like you* to the tour guide,

would that make us sacrilegious
or honest? When he asks you, not me,

if we are engaged or married,
you say *yes*

to him because I also agree
that's more convenient. Does that read

it's inconvenient to be me –
too young, too female,

too Asian? Forgive me, I am letting
history talk over my heartache –

next to souvenir stalls, sick of
the millionth photo of one important leader

shaking hands with other important leaders,
we stop holding hands too.

Silence

KITEC Hong Kong, 2011

At Mogwai's gig, a girl,
armed with a belt
of Yakult,
danced
and

        knocked
        onto me.

                The bottled lager
                I was drinking
                chipped the
                tip of my
                tooth –

                all

        I heard
        was a ringing
        through my skull,

                    sheltering
                    me
                    within

                    the wall
                    of sound.

Happiness

comes like an ambulance
you hear from a distance.
You were once told that
you don't miss a person.
You miss the period they represent.
What they were trying to say was
we're over.   In bed,
you re-watch *The Reader*,
and think *why can't life*
feel like the towel
between Hannah and Michael
when she presses her body,
naked, against his.

      This has to happen
in the summer of things.
The times you visit Berlin,
someone unexpected
becomes your need.
Outside Friedrichstraße station,
the air is different.
Someone has revealed its fictions:
even old seats, stale piss
from the nights before
pry you open.
      You notice the siren
for the first time, wafting
outside Michael's room.
You've heard it in person,
piercing as fluorescent orange
down Boddinstraße.
      Nine years since, you've
finally learned to say,
I've missed you and
I'm done with abstractions.

Muscle Memory

Courage is a half-rehearsed song.
You, you, you, you are the notes.

How we brush shoulders at a bar
then outside headquarters.

How you care enough to say *hi,*
briefly taking off your mask.

How we trespass
mountains, hedges, highways...

How you push twigs to make way
so I, marching behind you,

won't be slapped in the face.
How we dot and dot open fields,

homing our horizons.
How lonely it is to choose –

you make it less so,
so I choose, over and over,

to not turn away,
to love you better in public.

意色樓 An Id Signal

————————————————Before amplifiers————black beehives
My innards shake like egg yolks——————————*Burn taa*——————
————————————————————*Bite taa*————*Breathe taa*——
Ah Lai becomes a wailing instrument————————————
————————————————*Words push ahh pull ahh edge into sounds*

Tones – meanings – abolished—————*Faa*——————————
————————————*Bloomed*————*unretained*—————
————————————————*Faa*——————————
In technicoloured haze————————————————
————————————*Big – tilted shadows flicker from wall to ceiling*

——————————*In doubts —— ize*————————————
————————————————*Lose pace —— ify* —————
——————————————————————————*Gathered then gone*
Shoe-gazers drink limelights————————————————
————————————————*Scattered through a forest of legs*

————*Moshers drag girls with school bags away* ——————
————————————————————*From the ring of speed*
——————————*Head-bangers wear the sore like a trophy*————
Vapourised at the singularity ————————————
————————————*Of sweat——booze——and smoke*————

Hidden Agenda

Then muffled riffs escaped industrial buildings.
    Indie kids smoked downstairs, knowing faces before names.

Then, as the lift went up, latticed sliding gates grunted.
Ghostly notes whirled, sharpened
        through the steel and concrete of each floor.

Then our hands stamped like livestock.
        Stickers, posters thickened all surfaces but the stage.

Then Nicole refused to play until Wai Ching,
            sent backstage, came round.
A metalhead, who wore only black, loved strawberry cakes.

Then toilets were half a phone booth. The door read:
*if you don't flush, your genital will turn to mush ^.^*

Then it's 1am and 14 missed calls.
    Matcha swiss rolls dyed my sick green.

Then I was *against all authorities, except for my mum*'s curfew.
    Looping *ha / ha / ha / ha / ha / can we get back together.*

Then the raids.

Then I blamed my lack of conviction on those who stopped me.
            I blamed my lack of conviction.
        I blamed my lack.

            Then I,

then I,

then I make I an anti-elegy,
then I make –

Bad Tattoo Poem

Channelling The Monkey King

No one could tame me –
born from a rock,
        brought havoc to heaven,
ate all the peaches.

I shapeshifted,
rode clouds
        beyond the edge of the universe,
Buddha's looming palm.

No one could tame me –
not those plump fingers
        of a mountain
plunging from the sky.

Not those hundreds of years
as I waited for release,
        feasted on dew and wind,
weeds burgeoned from my holes.

O my hairless child,
what have you done, led through
        karaoke, Tsingtao beer swills,
the night bus to Shenzhen?

My image blasted on your back
for the price of a cheap cell phone.
        Contour dimmed into bruises.
Fur, burnt matches.

A bad copy of mine
is enough to scar.
        No one could tame me –
black me out – I gnarl.

Notes

Languages: Throughout the book, I used Chinese characters (some shared between Mandarin and Cantonese, some differed); 拼音 pinyin (the official romanisation of Mandarin); 粵拼 jyutping (the official romanisation of Cantonese); and loose transliteration of Cantonese and Hokkien. Choices were context-dependent. Where I thought mispronunciation and obscurity (to non-Mandarin/Cantonese/Hokkien users) were key to the poem, I used Chinese characters or loose transliteration. Where accurate pronunciations aided the musicality of the poem, I used pinyin or jyutping. The numbers in jyutping indicated the tones in Cantonese. Dictionaries are available on Google.

I didn't force standardisation in the book as an attempt to reflect Hong Kong's hybrid languages. In daily digital communication, Hongkongers might opt for loose transliterations of Cantonese characters that are between jyutping and English. A quick example would be the name 盧亭. It is Lou⁴ Ting⁴ in jyutping; Lo Ting in loose transliteration. For proper nouns as such, the latter romanisation strikes me as more immediately recognisable. If you are interested, 謝曉虹 Dorothy Tse's essay 'Writing Between Languages' (2011) points out the complexity of what is considered to be "mother tongue" in Hong Kong writing.

'Girl Ghosts' is after *Some Girls Walk into the Country They Are From* (2020) by Sawako Nakayasu.

'The Birth of a New Hero' is titled after Tung Ming-Chin's sculpture *The Birth of a New Hero* (2008). The poem also borrows a phrase from '秦皇島 (Qinhuangdao)' by 萬能青年旅店 (Omnipotent Youth Society).

'After *Isla*' takes inspiration from Yoan Capote's *Isla* (see-escape).

'Lantau (Rotten Head)' & **'Deluge'**: Under British colonial rule, Lantau became the romanised name of an area in Hong Kong. It used to be called 'Laan¹ Tau⁴' by villagers, which translates directly as Rotten Head. The area was a site of many revolutions against Chinese dynasties, where bodies of soldiers and villagers were found. Despite opposition and controversy, Lantau's water is to undergo a large-scale reclamation project in partnership with Chinese companies. The project, titled Lantau

Tomorrow Vision, is to spend half of Hong Kong's fiscal reserves to build housing units that will be available in 30 years the soonest.

'**Emergency Regulations Ordinance (1922-)**' quotes Winston Churchill and Gershom Stewart from the digitised editions of Commons and Lords Hansard, the Official Report of debates in Parliament. Words in brackets are from accounts of protesters in 2019, some of whom were arrested under the 1922 ordinance. The poem's form is inspired by Gail McConnell's *The Sun is Open*.

'**Yau Teng Daughters**' plays with origin stories of naming step daughters in Cantonese based on the name's tonal differences.

'**Salt and Rice**"s last line alludes to 《海浪裏的鹽：香港九十後世代訪談故事》 by 蔡寶賢. The poem is mostly made of Cantonese idioms directly translated into English.

Poems titled '**The Tattoo Collector**' are inspired by articles "Ötzi the Iceman: What we know 30 years after his discovery" (*National Geographic*); "How Tattoos Saved These Indonesian Women From Sexual Slavery In World War II" (*VICE*).

'瑞龍樓 **Shui Lung House**' contains lines from a Mandarin nursery rhyme. They could be translated as: 'little lamb, be good, be good / open, open the door / come, come / mama is back'.

'**Florence and the Machine**' is after the form of Tiana Clark's 'BBHMM'.

'**Re:** *Do you feel guilty for not writing in your mother tongue?*' is after Laura Williams' photography collection 'INVISIBLE'.

'**Hidden Agenda**' is titled by the namesake of a legendary music venue in Hong Kong.

'**My Bloody Galentines**' adapts a conversation I had with Medha Singh; '**Happiness**', a phrase from Ramya Chamalie Jirasinghe's poem 'No Looking Back: Everyone's Memoir', '**Lantau (Rotten Head)**', a phrase from Hala Alyan's Instagram posts on Palestinian resistance and stories as told by Sally and Rex, a couple who divide their time between the land and sea; '**What do you do with a stone**', a phrase from Lola Olufemi's *Experiment in Imagining Otherwise* (2021); '**Faces and Masks**', a paragraph from Eduardo Galeano's *Faces and Masks* (1984) and Adrienne Rich's

A Wild Patience Has Taken Me This Far (1981); '**Rudimentary Cantonese**', a line from '春曉 A Spring Morning' by 孟浩然 Meng Haoran; '意色樓 **An Id Signal**', my creative translation of the word "化" in the band's lyrics '剎那快慰 (Volatile Consolation)'; '**Hidden Agenda**', lyrics of HTRK's 'Ha' and a phrase from Padraig Regan's 'Poem for Bobby Kendall'; '**Master Narratives**', phrases from Qu Qiubai's essay 'On translation – A letter to Lu Xun (1931)' in Leo Tak-hung Chan's Book *Twentieth-Century Chinese Translation Theory* (2004); '**Death Accents**', Franny Choi's 'In the morning I scrolled my way back into America' and Emma Must's discussion on *Out of Time: Poetry from the Climate Emergency* (Ed. by Kate Simpson) (2021) at Verve Poetry Festival; '**What have you thrown away**', a prompt from Samuel Tongue's workshop on Ecopoetics at Push The Boat Out Festival; '**Muscle Memory**', bell hook's idea on 'choosing' in *All About Love: New Visions* (1999) and a phrase from Sanah Ashan's essay 'Allowing Our Hearts To Break: Poetry, Our Embodied Method of Resistance' in *Too Little / Too Hard* (Issue 2); 'Bad Tattoo Poem', a phrase from Alan Gillis's 'The Magus'.

Acknowledgements

People I thanked in my pamphlet, *Tapping At Glass* (Verve, 2023), still stand. Additional thanks to Southbank Centre New Poets Collective 2022/23 for the genuine and generous conversations. This book is supported by Scottish Book Trust's Ignite Fellowship and Arts Council England's Develop Your Creative Practice (DYCP) Grant.

Thank you, Jane Commane, for trusting, editing and promoting this book. When you said you remembered one of the poems from an online workshop you and Jennifer Wong co-delivered five years ago, I knew I found the right publisher.

Thank you, Jay Gao and Niall Campbell, for the mentorship when I got lost in earlier versions of this book (Panic! In the [last minute] emails).

Thank you, Au Wah Yan, for a short speech you forgot you made in Choi Yuen Village's 拆到爛哂音樂嘉年華 thirteen years ago. That changed my teenage views on anger and care. I feel so honoured and pampered for your designing my book covers.

Thank you, Felix Chow and Eric Yip, for your edits and suggestions.

Poems have appeared (some drastically rewritten) in the following journals, magazines, and/or platforms: *Gutter, Poetry London, Voice and Verse Poetry Magazine, Bad Lilies, Under the Radar, Berlin Lit, Tupelo Quarterly, The Tiger Moth Review, Berfrois, Litter, Poetry, Cordite, diode, The Common, Canto Cutie,* theHythe, *PN Review, Wildness, From Arthur's Seat,* BBC Scotland, *Cicada, Suspect (Singapore Unbound), The Hong Konger, Our Time Is A Garden* (IASH), *Rabbit Poetry, WrICE Anthology* (Bowen Street Press & RMIT)*, Dreich, The Rialto, Irish Pages, The London Magazine* and *Perverse.* Six poems in this book were in my oversized pamphlet *Tapping At Glass* (Verve, 2023).

'Blue Fires', 'What do you do with a stone?', and 'Muscle Memory' are commissioned by The Edinburgh Futures Institute. They are part of a collaborative performance. Thank you, Ioannis Kalkounos, for the invitation. It helped me metabolise the significance of Hong Kong's movements. Thank you, Pippa Murphy. Your expertise in music composition helped me redraft the pieces. Watch the performance here: https://vimeo.com/875096239

Thank you, dear reader, for spending time with this book. I am mostly confused. Sharing helps me cope with that.